Principled Leadership;
A Balancing Act for a Lifetime

Principled Leadership;
A Balancing Act for a Lifetime

Also by Glenn Jackson

Surviving the Radicalization of America

Growing Leadership; Managing Developmental Chaos

The Siege At Azulon

Principled Leadership;
A Balancing Act for a Lifetime

Glenn Jackson

Principled Leadership;
A Balancing Act for a Lifetime

Glenn Jackson

Contact via email at: growingleadership@live.com

ISBN 13: 978-0-615-67845-0

Cover Art: I completed this several years ago. It
is titled, Balancing Act. The idea of the work is
that we are standing precariously in the midst of
turmoil and chaos. The goal is to maintain
balance as we confront the chaos and change we
find around us, that is pulling and pushing us
in different directions. Only by having full
awareness of self can someone effectively
balance through this storm of life. That is, to a
large degree, principled leadership.

Principled Leadership;
A Balancing Act for a Lifetime

To my loving wife, Kristina; you inspire me each
and every day through your courage, strength
and passion.
Thank you for your friendship and love.

Principled Leadership;
A Balancing Act for a Lifetime

Principled Leadership;
A Balancing Act for a Lifetime

Table of Contents

Item   **Page**

Introduction   11

Chapter 1, It Has to Start Somewhere: 15

"Nothing is stronger than principle. No other concept has the quality, integrity or characteristic of principle. Principles are those beliefs we stand upon. Principles are the rocks that do not move in the storm. Principles are powerful. Principles last forever."

Chapter 2, Pre-Construction: 39

"The foundation of leadership then is laid courageously and is strengthened through continuously enhanced and attained wisdom. Wisdom, in turn, is reinforced and strengthened through the behavior of living virtuously."

Chapter 3, Construction: 69

"They seem to believe that becoming a

believer in God is the wrong path to take, because they see it as a limiting factor in their life and a marginal belief, rather than the unlimited spiritual experience that it actually is."

Chapter 4, Post-Construction: 101

"The fruit of your life is the virtue you show in life. This is created through living your life based on positive values that are tempered through wisdom and lived courageously. This is the journey, not simply to attain this state of existence, but to sustain it. In essence, this is the path that must always be following, because staying on the path is living principled leadership."

Chapter 5, Sharing Value Systems: 115

"As an example, the value of being honest is unchanging. Either you are being honest or you are not. Truth does not change. We cannot therefore say we are changing the value of honesty. In

*essence, to change the meaning or value
of honesty means to be dishonest."*

Chapter 6, Living Principled Leadership: 134
*"If the human being is the apex of
existence, then God cannot exist. If God
cannot exist, then the foundation of our
values cannot exist. If our values cannot
exist, then we have human centric chaos
and descent into anarchy."*

Bibliography: 150

Principled Leadership;
A Balancing Act for a Lifetime

Principled Leadership;
A Balancing Act for a Lifetime

Introduction

First and foremost, I believe in and have complete faith in God. I find that no other experience, thought or attitude yields the good fruit or energy in the manner that this belief delivers. Some argue that we are able to establish virtue and live good values without this belief. While I cannot say that this is not true, I can say that I have found that personal belief has given me access to a certain spiritual power that provides me a means to a perception of the divine that I believe is real and valuable in growing spiritually and living a value based life.

Without this spiritual power that exists through the divinity of belief, the values that could be established are human centric values. While human centric values are not all necessarily bad (think of being nice to each other, providing shelter, food, safety, etc.), there is a certain hollowness in the idea of value without divine inspiration. To me, value absent belief is a weak or temporary state. Contrarily, belief, although a stumbling block for some people, is the key to unlock the potential that exists through the spiritual connection to God and the values that are found through that belief.

To be sure, I am not an active member of any established religion, although I was raised Christian, as a Protestant in the Methodist Church. For this reason, you will find that the quotations that I use are basically from the Bible. However, I have read large segments of books in the Vedic tradition, including the Bhagavad Gita. I have also read large sections of the Koran and philosophies of Plato, Nietzsche, Augustine, Descartes, Confucius and others. I have also meditated, read other works, studied theology and history; and have reached what I believe are my own conclusions.

I am not active in politics, although I have contributed to various political groups and causes over the years and occasionally write a letter to the editor. However, I do believe my country and our species for that matter, is seriously on the wrong track and that we need to do something to change our course.

The something I see as a true need today that would help us change course is to find that

Principled Leadership;
A Balancing Act for a Lifetime

balance we need between our physical and our spiritual life. While much is written that focuses on our physical environment, a return to those principles that represent the fundamental values we have learned over time would bring us back to a balanced approach to life. To accomplish this I believe we need to relearn and embrace those values that are based on the principles we learned through a stronger spiritual connection.

A step toward this would be to establish these principles in and as a fundamental element of our personal, corporate and political leadership. I don't mean we should elect politicians who only adhere to a certain religion or that religious leaders should be our national leaders. I am not talking about religion. I simply mean we need to return to personal character that is based on those values that are spiritually based and provide us the balance we need in order to effectively live all aspects of our life.

The values we find that are spiritually inspired are positive in all undertakings. Following those values in our leadership development and active life can only yield enhanced and improved leadership performance. This performance is what we need to change the course of our nation's and our species current trajectory into the future.

This book is designed then, to discuss the balance between our spirit and physical reality, and the power to be found in the principles we learned through a stronger spiritual connection and the values we derive from them as a foundation for effective principled leadership.

Principled Leadership;
A Balancing Act for a Lifetime

Chapter 1

It Has to Start Somewhere

You are reading this book because you are interested in leadership. In that, we share a certain thing in common, because I, too, am interested in leadership; but more importantly, I am interested in the values that support leadership. Even more importantly, I am interested in how we can bring balance back into our lives and apply this to leadership by embracing the spiritual aspect of our existence through understanding, exploring, and embracing the principles of those spiritual values we have learned over time. These values should be applied as the tools to enable us to create a stronger foundation for our life in general. Harnessing the power of these values should also provide us the ability to establish and live a life of principled leadership.

One important point to keep in mind as you read this book – this is not a political book. While I know political leadership is a topic that is near and dear to everyone, since it involves the direction for our country and our world, that is not the subject of this book. This book is about the principles, values and fundamentals of character that founds leadership, and any individual, regardless of party affiliation can demonstrate and live principled leadership.

Before we delve into principled leadership let's take a step back and look at leadership from a more generic perspective so we can establish some commonality of understanding.

- <u>Leadership</u>

Leadership is an intriguing concept. There are countless books written about it; we know it when we see it; we certainly know it when it is applied incorrectly; we don't truly understand exactly how to get it; we don't really know if we can or how to give it to someone else; we really don't understand exactly what it is; we each seem to understand it differently; we are not sure if it is better naturally occurring or if it should be developed through training; and we believe a leader can provide us with competent guidance, safety and security. It is an interesting set of characteristics that include more than these few. But because of the complexity of leadership and the many uncertainties of it, we often misunderstand leadership.

One of the biggest reasons for this misunderstanding appears to be the manner in which we perceive leadership. We seem to perceive leadership to be a singularity rather than a plurality. Simply put, it appears that we often develop leadership skill with a definitive goal in mind rather than a set of competencies, values and learning's that can establish a fundamental position from which we can not only lead a team, but from which we can establish leadership principles for our entire life.

This variance in how we perceive leadership is critical because it drives not only our understanding of it, but our processes to use it, train it and apply it. A singular use training program that takes someone to a room and teaches them how to apply certain actions to achieve certain results is not actually teaching leadership, but that is what we call it.

Principled Leadership;
A Balancing Act for a Lifetime

For example, we provide leadership training for many singular needs – the leader of a team, section, group, office or company – which is defined purpose leadership. This is what I call single use leadership, and while it is not bad, it is only partial leadership and is not lasting because it is more attuned to the needs of a certain group of people or a defined business process rather than the larger process of growing internal leadership competency for life.

I have seen this in multiple settings, where individuals who are promoted to a supervisory or management position are sent to a class to "learn leadership." The things they teach at these classes are usually designed and targeted to the specific role or position the individuals in the group are moving into. While this is a good start, it is limited in that it only provides minimal discussion of skills and knowledge needed by individuals for those positions.

In this we don't seem to drive people to understand the values that leadership is founded upon. These values, such as honesty, cannot be taught in a classroom but must be societal values that are part of the fiber or fabric of the individual. However, without continuing to teach them and express or reinforce their importance, these critical values can get lost in the drive to perform.

While leadership is not something that can be learned in a book or classroom, the basic concepts and ideas can be explored and utilized. But leadership competency takes experience and guidance to be properly learned and effectively applied. Even more importantly, the values that establish the foundation of leadership must be reaffirmed and taught as the critical learning's of effective positive leadership. Only by constantly reinforcing these primary values will we be able to establish a paradigm of principles as the major drivers for our actions as leaders.

Another failure of some of these leadership development processes is that most people don't even get these single use leadership classes. In this case, most people are not exposed to leadership development except as it is applied to them, rather than a skill they develop and grow. For this reason it is even more imperative that we find the means and take the time to reaffirm the importance of the fundamental values that support leadership.

As mentioned, the single use leadership process usually focuses on the business or employment aspect of leadership, but it does not get into the personal leadership necessary to effectively sustain leadership for life. In most cases the conversations do not get into basic values that support leadership, nor do they discuss value systems that support group dynamics.

Understand that single use leadership development is a whole lot better than no exposure to leadership at all. Even when these classes discuss leadership it involves the interaction with people and establishing relationships. These are positive conversations and help in the development process, but they are limiting in that they simply do not go far enough.

Leadership training even at the basic level needs to encompass not only the immediate business needs of the training and the further individual development of the person, but the larger discussion of group dynamics, values as tools to establish character, principles and wisdom. Many training courses simply do not have enough time to spend the time necessary to do this, working to practice immediate need skills for application in the working environment.

Another failing of our perception of leadership is that we seem to view leadership in the present tense instead of in a moving past/present/future tense. Leadership is not something that only exists now, because leadership binds what we learned from past experience and our expectations of the future into a cohesive thought or action, and is accomplished by steps taken in the present as a movement toward the future. Leadership is a time traveler. For this reason alone, leadership must be flexible and versatile to embrace change. We cannot therefore simply view leadership as a present tense skill; instead we must view it as a movement and cross time skill.

I know of no other concept that is designed to bridge the gap between the present and future in the manner that leadership is designed. It makes leadership a unique and

Principled Leadership;
A Balancing Act for a Lifetime

critically important skill. Remember that leaders are there to take us forward into the future. People don't provide leadership to look to the past and leadership is not simply a skill to manage right now situations, although that can be a big part of it. Leadership is about the movement of people through time. That is what a vision is all about – a goal that is far enough out to be nearly tangible, but always a little further than can be actually completed. Leaders use this to gather energies and competencies of people and help them move toward the future goal willingly.

Even at a small level this is leadership. Take a small team of 15 people. The leader does not simply talk about how the team performed or is performing, but discusses trends that have been developed over time, ties it to the current performance level and provides ideas, suggestions and a vision to impact performance into the future. This is a time expanding concept. This is taking people from the known into the unknown with a level of certainty and positive expectation.

Principled Leadership;
A Balancing Act for a Lifetime

Also, leadership isn't created in and doesn't exist in a vacuum, nor is it isolated to the specific silo of the minimum definition. It takes much more.

Leadership is:

- created with courage,
- sustained through wisdom,
- built on values,
- established through character,
- energized with virtue, and,
- demonstrated with passion.

You do not get all of these to coalesce through accidental events or a business leadership course. Leadership is purposeful. I believe that leadership built through this process can be principled leadership. The question then is not how do we grow leadership, but how do we grow so we can live a life defined as principled leadership? Good question.

- Principle

But before we move forward to a deeper discussion of leadership and structure, we need to discuss an additional item that harnesses the intent of this book. That item is principle. The definition is: *"NOUN; 1. basic assumption: an important underlying law or assumption required in a system of thought; 2. ethical standard: a standard of moral or ethical decision-making; 3. way of working: the basic way in which something works; 4. source: the primary source of something."*

A principle, the basic assumption; underlying law; ethical standard; the basic way it works; the primary source. These are clearly defining the fundamental, basic foundation. In regards to leadership, principle implies the very basic foundation upon which leadership rests. Principled leadership therefore is the term to describe the type of leadership that is grounded on fundamentally basic values that guide the choices made and the actions taken in the activity of providing and living leadership.

Nothing is stronger than principle. No other concept has the quality, integrity or characteristic of principle. Principles are those beliefs we stand upon. Principles are the rocks that do not move in the storm. Principles are powerful. Principles last forever.

Building leadership upon this type of principle defines someone. Principled leadership is the strongest type of leadership. This is leadership that does not move in the storm, but that is powerful and lasts forever. This is the type of leadership we need in order to drive towards establishing balance back into our society. This is the type of leadership that builds and sustains a strong structure.

- A Strong Structure

In order to create anything that lasts a long time, a structure must be well built out of good materials in a safe location in a manner so as to resist most expected events that would try to destroy it. This seems to be a fairly straightforward concept.

One of the problems we have today is that we have not developed the support systems in our culture well enough to assist people who are trying to achieve this goal.

- We have training development classes – then basically push people to learn and figure it out themselves.

- We give some lip service to the discussion of values as things to embrace in order to be a good leader – but we do not make it a primary need in our culture or a primary training goal of our development courses.

- We talk about energy and motivation – then overwhelm people with unrealistic expectations.

- We speak praises for people who excel in business, school, music, sports, etc. – but we focus on people's natural performance ability instead of their actual demonstrated character.

- We sing praises for leaders who visibly achieve profit and performance goals for themselves and their team – but do not provide examples of leaders who selflessly demonstrate outstanding leadership characteristics.

- We front page political leaders who take various positions on the issues – but we do not discuss the leadership characteristics or value systems that make them the leader we are discussing.

- We say we believe in God, but seem to do more and more as a culture and society to push God out of our conversation and public life than bring Him in.

- We embrace technology in everything we do – but we ignore the spirit to our peril.

So how do we "create anything that lasts a long time," in regards to leadership? As a first step, I believe we have to better understand what leadership is. Until we truly have a grasp on exactly what we are working to establish, we simply cannot understand how that item can be made to be lasting.

This is important, because leadership affects every one of us. Whether we consciously pay attention to it or not, leadership does, in one way or another, have a direct impact on nearly every aspect of our lives. The taxes we pay, our wages, our international relationships, religious institutions, wars, our laws, costs for goods and services, what is provided through entertainment, what is taught in school, the speed limit, cost of bread – all of these and more are determined by someone or a group of people filling leadership functions.

- Leadership Defined

As defined, leadership is a noun, and means the following: *"The position or function of a leader; ability to lead; an act or instance of leading; guidance; direction; the leaders of a group."* It can be expanded through the addition of the definitions of leading, which is an adjective, meaning *"directing or guiding"*; and leader, which is a noun that means *"a person or thing that leads or a guiding or directing head, as of an army, movement, or political group."*

This is a very good starting point, but even when you add up all three definitions they still miss out on what I believe to be some critical aspects of leadership, to include:

1) The substantial effect leadership has on the people being led,

2) The actual process of determining effective leadership action, and,

3) The focus on leadership's core principles.

In order to bridge that gap and create a comprehensive and mutually understood definition of the term leadership and to ensure we share an understanding of the enormity of power placed within leadership, here is my expanded definition.

Leadership, in addition to the dictionary definition above, *"is the expressive word that describes the characteristics of the individual or group of people executing the process of leading people from their current reality, through an uncertain future, to a perceived, mutually understood destination."* In this, leadership is the tool that focuses the power of expectation in the follower(s) to enable that follower(s) to believe his/her path through uncertainty is planned. Leaders are the ones who have the developed skill in harnessing this power and providing the focus necessary to complete the journey, as well as the confidence of the followers to get them there. This then establishes leadership as a mix of skill and confidence. The complexity of leadership is that these two items, skill and confidence, are independent of each other, but enormous when operating in synergy with each other.

For example, an individual may have great skill at planning and helping to achieve results, but if the people that should follow do not follow because they do not have confidence in the person, or if they think the person will take them in the wrong direction, they will not follow – leadership failure.

Or a person may truly be able to express the vision and people may truly believe in them and have confidence in them, but if that leader simply cannot figure out how to actually make the change happen, does not have the skill, people will become disenchanted and fall away – leadership failure.

However, when someone joins these two aspects together; provides the vision and sustaining energy necessary to achieve it and effectively establishes and outlines the steps necessary to get there; it allows people to follow with confidence at the highest level of synergy and delivers successful leadership.

Leadership then is both an incredibly powerful force and a skill with defined, measureable characteristics and results. Effective value based leadership is further defined as a positive application and not a negative one. The reason for this is that negative application has been observed in our history and while negative leaders have had lasting impacts, the leaders themselves have been defined as unhealthy for the greater good.

Hitler, Mussolini, Stalin, Hussein, just to name a few, had enormous impact on how we view leadership. But we all agree that they failed in the principled leadership category because they were overly selfish, biased and power hungry, among other traits. Leadership, in order to be clearly successful and lasting, cannot be any of those, as it ultimately prevents the followers from willingly committing their confidence to the leader.

Principled Leadership;
A Balancing Act for a Lifetime

This is where humanity branches. As we all move down the path of life, we see and follow our leaders. Leaders, as they move down the path, must choose directions to go. Some leaders have seen the branches in the road and have chosen the path that gave them:

- The best sense of personal security
- The most power
- The most money
- The most political gain

Still others have approached these branches and chosen to do what is best for the followers behind them. Why is there a difference?

The difference is in the values that are the foundation of each leader. A leader with core values that are weak or selfish will make those same choices. However, a leader with core values that are strong and positive will make the best choices for those affected by the choice. This is principled leadership.

- <u>Lasting</u>

Principled Leadership;
A Balancing Act for a Lifetime

I use the word "lasting" a lot in this book. The word lasting is a word of power. When we think of things that have lasted a long time we think of things like the pyramids. These monumental objects were built thousands of years ago and have lasted over time. It is powerful proof that something can be built by humans that can last a long time.

In the context of leadership, lasting implies leadership that lasts a life time. We should be able to understand and believe the epitaph: this leader did not stop leading, he passed on. We should be developing leadership qualities that are our habits that last all of our days. This is living a lasting principled leadership. Maintaining the principles and values of character, integrity and honesty for all of our days should be the focus of our leadership development from day one. We should not limit how we teach leadership to the singularity of a present business or process need.

What then, must someone be taught to be or learn to do in order for them to deliver this function effectively and for the long haul? What needs to done so we can "create anything that lasts a long time?" It is a good question with no easy answer, but it lends itself directly to the establishment of principled leadership.

- <u>Built to Last</u>

If you are building a structure that you want to last, you have to evaluate several items. These include building techniques, materials, architectural plans, available supply, cost, risk, manpower and location of the building. After all, you have to answer the why, where, when, what, who and how of all the steps. The same is true in the development of leadership.

Leadership is not an isolated or abstract phenomenon that is out there in kind of an ephemeral existence. Leadership has immediate impact. Leadership, in one respect, is a tangible performance standard based on a decision making process supported by the fundamental beliefs and knowledge of the holder. It is to the fundamental beliefs then that we must travel to see the foundation of the building. However, before you can begin to lay that foundation, you have to do some "pre-construction" work.

Principled Leadership;
A Balancing Act for a Lifetime

As mentioned, one of the items you must review before you build is simple: where are you going to build? This might seem like a silly question, but it is not. After all, you cannot build a foundation of leadership on shifting principles. You cannot build a foundation of leadership on uncertain values. There are some things you have to do first, which we will get to in a moment.

Also, as mentioned, you have to take a look at the building materials you have and determine if they are the right ones. For example, a foundation built with lies and deceit will not support effective positive leadership, so you need to get hold of material that will support your structure.

Once you have the foundation laid you need to determine what your framework will be. What framework can support good values? What is needed for values to be strong and secure? How strong should the framework be to withstand the violence and turmoil that life can generate and throw at you?

Simply stated, the framework you build must be proven to be strong enough to withstand the worst there is, even unto death. No other framework can be strong enough or good enough; because any framework that is not that strong will break.

Lastly, the values you attach to your framework, your structure, is the visible evidence of your character and your morality in action. It too must be strong. Your values then must also be lasting values. Embracing these values means both finding the ones that are powerful and understanding the true meaning and depth of each. So where do you start?

- Process

This book is designed to move through the process of the circle. I say that, because in essence, the only place you begin to find balance in your life and build lasting principled leadership is wherever you are, right now, as you read this book, so the circle begins now.
  - o If you have not actually begun to seek personal leadership, you have a tremendous amount of very hard and rewarding work to do.

Principled Leadership;
A Balancing Act for a Lifetime

○ If you have begun your journey and have started developing your personal leadership, you must keep going forward, but as you gain in wisdom, you will discover that there are things you need to go back to do while moving forward.

○ If you are a leader, you will discover that you need to review your foundation and framework in order to further sustain your structure and make sure your leadership is truly lasting leadership that is growing in wisdom courageously.

The easiest way to describe and work through this process is to create an analogy that supports the conversation. For that purpose I am using the analogy of building a home. The phases of this construction are:

➤ Pre-construction. This entails:

- Making the decision to build,
- Planning where to build, and,
- Evaluating the materials to use.

➤ Construction. This entails:

- The work of actually laying the foundation,
- Building the basic frame, and,
- Enclosing the structure.

> Post-construction. This entails:

- Moving into the house,
- Creating a home environment, and,
- Maintaining the created home.

The phases above are for reference to the process, but as we move through the conversation remember the actual discussion will be about getting into specific characteristics and values that lead to our ability to establish spiritual balance in life and grow living lasting principled leadership.

Chapter 2

Pre-Construction

In the previous chapter we discussed those items that would be considered in the "pre-construction" phase, which are those things you do before you actually begin the work of building. While this is true in the reality of building a house, it is slightly different in regards to the analogy of building the foundation of your life as you move toward establishing principled leadership. The difference, of course, is that the activity of pre-construction of a house has a defined beginning and a defined end. The activity of pre-construction as it relates to your life is different, because it begins wherever you are now in the path of life, not with a clean slate or clear blue-print with defined beginning or end points.

After all, you are already living your life. You already have life experiences, prejudices, perceptions, beliefs, learning and concepts. You have already done some of the things mentioned in this book or perhaps none/many of the things listed; but in any case, your journey has led you to the point where you now are. So as you begin this new home/life building process and make new discoveries about yourself, you will be creating the new from within the current values, principles and life that you currently live.

In many ways, this is harder than the simplicity of building an actual house. It is harder to discover new and create it within when you are who you are and have established your place based upon who you have perceived yourself to be for all of the time you have been. This is an arena of very tough choices and hard work. So where do you begin?

- Courage

"Courage is action in the face of fear."

When I penned those words in my previous leadership book, *Growing Leadership; Managing Developmental Chaos,* I was focused primarily on the process of growing leadership and creating the energy necessary to do things that a person would not normally do, in the context of leadership development in the work environment. However, the need for courage in the action of developing and living principled leadership is even stronger.

Courage truly is an engine of power and someone who has courage can achieve things that several other people cannot. Courage is powerful and it is bigger than the development phase, so it is a foundational element necessary to successfully complete all the steps in this book and to live a full life that is balanced spiritually and focused on principled leadership. This is because it takes courage to:

- o Hold yourself accountable for your own behavior.
- o Keep your commitment to stay the course.
- o Not lower your standards.
- o Not lose focus on your priorities.
- o Not take life for granted.
- o Not be complacent.
- o Not go along to get along.
- o Look at yourself, be honest with yourself and realize that you have

significant work required, and then to follow through with that change.

Courage is certainly a personal trait that anyone seeking leadership must possess. But is courage the source of energy only a youth needs to attain leadership? – Absolutely not. Courage is a source of power that not only enables growth into leadership, but sustains the values and characteristics that make principled leadership possible. Without continued courage, leadership falters. However, courage used without wisdom can eventually become wasted energy and can only be sustained for a time.

A leader who exhibits courage in strength of character, decisions and energy; who is not afraid to get out front and lead; can only go so far if she is not gaining in wisdom through lessons learned in life. Being courageous but making the same repeated mistakes eventually wastes the energy of courage, because people will begin to not follow someone who is apparently neither learning nor applying wisdom.

Courage does remain a necessary force as we age and grow in wisdom. But it is courage coupled with wisdom that creates and sustains our ability to balance our life and live principled leadership.

A leader infused with wisdom that is courageous in leadership will be amplified and strengthened through the wisdom gained. This is the role of wisdom in leadership.

When beginning the journey of changing your life (building the house), it takes courage to make the decision to build. It means you are committing yourself to a tough quest for an outcome that may not be what you expect, is fraught with problems and challenges, and requires continuous effort to achieve.

Courage, in this context, is one of the primary items needed to make the decision to begin. Without it, most people simply think about the idea or they wish they could, but they don't actually take action to do it. As Yoda said in Star Wars, *"Try not. Do. Or do not. There is no try."* Courage is the difference between wishing and doing.

Principled Leadership;
A Balancing Act for a Lifetime

- Wisdom

    Discussing wisdom is the first step in the discussion of the individual items of building material that becomes our personal character. This will tie directly into the value that is the created house (self) of the project. Wisdom is the first essential foundational building block, because wisdom is the deepest, highest or richest (depending on how you perceive it) level of learning about life any of us can attain. The choices we make are determined by the level of wisdom we possess. Living principled leadership is directly proportional to the level of wisdom grasped.

    However, wisdom is not something that either comes easy or that is found quickly. For that reason, everyone who journeys towards principled leadership must be courageous and should understand that wisdom is an attribute to attain along the journey. Wisdom is not an attribute at the beginning of the quest for leadership, but one that is arrived at through patience, trial and error, time and distance, seeking and learning. Yet wisdom is an attribute that must be in the forefront of thought and desire at all times. It is the effort to attain wisdom, through consciously seeking it, that gives wisdom the essential value it possesses. It is the wisdom gained that gives it significant power and strength.

This unique place wisdom holds in the task of building a balanced life that supports principled leadership is the primary reason principled leadership's pursuit is a cycle.

> ➤ If you are beginning the quest, much is to be worked on and experienced before wisdom begins to be revealed.

> ➤ If you have attained a certain balance in your spiritual life and are performing in a level of leadership, you should know that wisdom is revealed slowly over time, so you continuously look to learn wisdom to reinforce and further support your foundation.

Regardless of where you are in the journey to leadership, wisdom constantly modifies the journey. But what is it?

The dictionary defines wisdom as: *"–noun: the quality or state of being wise; knowledge of what is true or right coupled with just judgment as to action; sagacity, discernment, or insight; scholarly knowledge or learning: the wisdom of the schools: wise sayings or teachings; precepts; a wise act or saying; the wisdom of Solomon."* This is a good beginning, but it needs context.

Some have asked, "What is wisdom and how do you get it?" In the book of Proverbs, the Wisdom of Solomon, he discusses many aspects of wisdom and provides a very good place to begin the discussion. I believe the following excerpt specifically, from chapter 2, verse 1 – 15, provides a significant starting place for seeking wisdom.

"My son, if you accept my words and store up my commands within you, turning your ear to wisdom and applying your heart to understanding— indeed, if you call out for insight and cry aloud for understanding, and if you look for it as for silver and search for it as for hidden treasure, then you will understand the fear of the LORD and

find the knowledge of God. For the LORD gives wisdom; from his mouth come knowledge and understanding. He holds success in store for the upright; he is a shield to those whose walk is blameless, for he guards the course of the just and protects the way of his faithful ones. Then you will understand what is right and just and fair—every good path. For wisdom will enter your heart, and knowledge will be pleasant to your soul. Discretion will protect you, and understanding will guard you. Wisdom will save you from the ways of wicked men, from men whose words are perverse, who have left the straight paths to walk in dark ways, who delight in doing wrong and rejoice in the perverseness of evil, whose paths are crooked and who are devious in their ways."

Principled Leadership;
A Balancing Act for a Lifetime

This is an excellent context to understand not only the value of wisdom, but the effort needed in order to find and grasp it. Wisdom is not something that is quickly learned, and is not something that comes without effort. Nor is wisdom an attribute that always remains part of your character without conscious effort. Importantly, even several thousand years ago wisdom was highly valued.

One reason wisdom is valued is that it is not something that is passed down from one to another. We get our hair color through our genes, but we don't get wisdom that way. Each generation and each person has to make the conscious effort to gain wisdom. Additionally, it is important to understand and recognize the reality that the world we live in today attempts to prevent us from gaining wisdom. That is because today our culture view's knowledge and information as superior to wisdom. Why is that?

It is a long story that involves a discussion of history. However, this book is not intended to provide a detailed account of the years of our history, so suffice to say that there was a slow development over time of increasing interest in the world around us, how it worked, what it was made of, why things behaved in certain ways, and a host of other questions. We even became aware of ourselves and the difference between good and evil.

Eventually, universities were established, research began and even with the turmoil of conflicts between the church and science, the scientific method was established.

This led to even more discovery as a good evaluative process was in place and we learned more and more about the physical world around us. Eventually, this led to increased application as technology, which continued to increase both knowledge and improve technology. In the evolution of this discovery and application process, the spiritual aspect of our humanity was gently but firmly pushed further and further aside as religious or "church" oriented, and perceived by the intelligentsia as irrelevant to the greater understanding of our existence. We have now reached that point where we appear to try and actively diminish the value of spiritual wisdom as nothing other than old, out of date knowledge.

However, wisdom is not and never has been simply "old knowledge." Nor is wisdom tied exclusively to a religion or church. Wisdom is not something that you discover through technology or science, nor is wisdom a collection of material possessions, higher education or the latest "app." While all of the off-shoots of our scientific quest and technological achievements are treasured in our society, they are not wisdom.

Wisdom comes from seeking spiritual truth and seeking understanding. Wisdom comes after you establish an attitude of personal searching and acknowledgement of place in the universe; a reverence for the divine in all things. Wisdom is focused on the conscious act of seeking and understanding and is the foundation of personal value. Wisdom looks inside to find the connection to God as the divine power of the universe.

Wisdom looks outside to understand how the human condition intertwines with the divine in all things. Wisdom is the internal quality of having sought it and gained it. Wisdom looks beneath the surface, not at the superficiality of the wants and desires of the current age. Wisdom seeks to understand the deeper meaning of self, not the obfuscation of self that is found through technology and science.

Wisdom is never out dated, because wisdom is always alive right now. Wisdom looks at deeper spiritual understanding, relationships and how they impact long-term viability, understanding how children mature and grow and the need for nurturing and discipline, understanding the human condition and how best to positively impact that. To say wisdom is only an old relic of a bygone belief in God era clearly demonstrates the lack of wisdom of the speaker.

- Virtue

The foundation of leadership then is laid courageously and is strengthened through continuously enhanced and attained wisdom. Wisdom, in turn, is reinforced and strengthened through the behavior of living virtuously. The only significant and valuable personal values that exist in leadership rest upon virtue, because while anyone can claim their values reflect their perspective or behavior, only someone who is wise and seeks virtue can live personal values that are based on the right foundation, and living virtuously requires courage.

Virtue is the key critical aspect of personal values. The definition of virtue is: *"virtue –noun: moral excellence; goodness; righteousness; conformity of one's life and conduct to moral and ethical principles; uprightness; rectitude; chastity; virginity: to lose one's virtue; a particular moral excellence; a good or admirable quality or property: the virtue of knowing one's weaknesses; effective force; power or potency; virtues, an order of angels; manly excellence; valor.*

- *Cardinal virtue: anything considered to be an important or characteristic virtue: Tenacity is his cardinal virtue;*
- *Ancient Philosophy- justice, prudence, temperance, and fortitude.*
- *Theological virtue: one of the three graces: faith, hope, or charity, infused*

into the human intellect and will by a special grace of god."

These are powerful internal values that each of us should strive to embrace. However, a stumbling block for many is that in order to live virtuously a person must subjugate the desires of the flesh and focus more on the desires of the spirit in order for these virtues to come alive. This is a key step in the path to living a balanced life that is capable of embracing principled leadership, and it is tough.

For example, the ability to subjugate self is a highly under-rated accomplishment, but one that is necessary to pursue virtue. What does it take to accomplish this? It takes many things, but essentially and primarily it takes the decision to do it. This is difficult by itself because in order to make this choice a person must choose to let things go that are currently valued, and having made this choice, it takes sacrifice, courage and hard work to actually achieve the result; a result that is constantly challenged in our culture, so on-going energy is required. It is a lifelong quest, not a short term task.

Principled Leadership;
A Balancing Act for a Lifetime

The virtues listed above are not easy to achieve, and in truth, most of us will not live most of them in the short time we have to work on it here. But we can have the attitude, heart and spirit to always be doing. This then places the act of living virtuously, even when falling short of success, at the forefront of success. This also provides clarity that seeking to live virtuously is the primary step toward the creation of personal values, and is the key to understanding the ensuing discussion of principled leadership in this book.

It is important to remember that for the remainder of the discussion in this book:

- When we discuss positive values, it is with the understanding that the courage exists to build the strong foundation that becomes the framework built with wisdom and strengthened by virtue that provides the fruitful evidence of its existence within the person.

- When we discuss values and value systems in general, it is with the understanding that they are only part of the system of mutual understanding and shared expectations we all share as a means to maintain a cohesive society based on those shared behaviors and shared expectations. While these shared values become value systems we all share, these values do not necessarily have a positive meaning, because they are not based on the foundation of wisdom, nor do they yield the fruit of virtue.

As I said, the effort to live virtuously is hard, as are all the steps in the growing and changing process.

- The knowledge that courage is required is valuable, but putting it to work is tougher.
- The knowledge that wisdom is critical to successfully balancing life and building principled leadership is valuable, but working and waiting to gain it is tougher.

- The knowledge that virtue is the fruit of your efforts is valuable, but living virtuously is tougher.

That brings up the subject of how and where you get the energy necessary to sustain your courage and move forward.

- <u>Motivation</u>

It takes energy to strive to live virtuously. It takes energy to be courageous. It takes energy to make tough decisions and live with them. I also recognize that this effort to grow and sustain principled leadership is not a process that is energized from external sources. That is not to say that temporary energy or reinforcement through a good motivational speaker will not give you a burst of energy and help you feel re-energized!

I have attended some very significant sessions over the years. I attended a workshop by Stephen Lundin on the *Fish!* philosophy, and I listened to Andy Andrews give a presentation on his book, *The Travelers Gift*. In both of these instances I was simply pumped up! They provided words and ideas that reached inside and opened the internal spigot of energy each of us must have and allowed me to feel totally energy filled. They were inspiring and just excellent moments.

But while experiences like this give you a boost and open your understanding and eyes to new concepts that can support you for the long term, the energy boost itself, as from any motivational speaker, is temporary, because it is external. Finding true energy requires you to understand your own motivation. The positive motivation for principled leadership is simple.

Motivation is the energy that dwells within that is tied to your values, character, goals and commitment to improve yourself and others.

Putting the concept into action is more complicated, because everyone is motivated. That may not sound right, but it is. Everyone is motivated, because everyone is living under the influence of the idea expressed above. Let's take it in pieces.

Principled Leadership;
A Balancing Act for a Lifetime

1. "Motivation is the energy that dwells within." This is true, as true lasting motivation can only come from within and it is within each person that motivations energy lives. However, the level of energy is different in each person. For example, some people's well seems to be empty, so the energy that dwells within is low. For these individuals it is nearly a reverse activity in that their well doesn't even seem to give but take. But even this negative motivation that takes their energy and seems to literally suck the life out of everything around them, is their motivational drive.

For those who have a strong reservoir of personal motivational energy within and have this spigot of energy open, the energy of self motivation is huge. Here is the energy a leader needs to do the right thing because it is the right thing to do, set the stage, be positive and motivational for others, have the energy to get the task complete, and courageously embrace principles and values. When properly aligned, it is a near limitless source of energy.

Regardless of your location on the scale of motivation, whether you are full spigot open or an empty well, you have to find the way to channel your motivational energy in order to be effective.

2. "Tied to your values and character." Everything in life is tied to your values and your character because every action you take or word you speak reveals your values and character. Your values and character are who you are. Positive character, for a leader, is critical and necessary in order for a leader to establish a trust followers can have in a leader. Because this is so critical, the energy of motivation ties directly to it and enhances the energy itself as well as the strength of the character so embraced.

However, this can be a negative asset as well, in that someone who has poor values and poor character but believe strongly in what they believe in will also find that well of energy inside to give their negative character energy. Energy is therefore a source that is not good or bad, it simply is. What you do with it and how you use it is defined by your values and your character.

3. "Goals and commitment to improve yourself and others." Everyone has goals, some

people just don't know what theirs are, while some people truly know what they are striving to achieve. Some people are engaged in short term goals, some in long term strategic goals. But in all cases, everyone has a goal. Like motivation, some goals are so well hidden from the person that they seem to have no goals or even negative goals.

The last piece of number three is commitment to improve yourself and others. This is the critical link that truly drives the purpose of leadership in the correct direction. Leadership that is energized and actively working to improve not only self but others as well, is positive leadership.

Principled leadership then is the action of holding your positive value based character in the well of your motivation, gaining strength to attain goals associated with improvement of yourself and those you lead. This action requires the balance of all these items to be effective. After all:

- Without values you have nothing to focus with.

- Without goals you have nowhere to take your motivational energy too.
- Without a purpose motivation is hollow.

Motivation provides the energy you get when you stand up for what is right because it is the right thing to do. Motivation provides the energy you need as the leader so you can stand up and provide the necessary guidance and vision for your team. Motivation provides the energy you need as the leader to face the tough decisions and take the responsibility for poor decisions or bad results. Motivation provides the energy to look inside and see that you have work to do in order to effectively provide leadership and be able to get the work done.

It is not easy being motivated. It requires purposeful thought and action. It requires bringing your awareness into focus and consciously making decisions about who you are, what you are doing and why you are doing it. Motivation requires the ability to channel your energy to conduct those steps necessary to support your character.

Maintaining your values in turn boosts your energy by providing the motivation to be strong in your character. It is a self fulfilling prophecy that as you grow stronger in your character you create more energy that strengthens your ability to maintain your character that creates energy... etc. This is good news, because leadership is hard.

Being a leader means you are in a place where you are expected to be aware of the strengths, weaknesses, opportunities and threats around you and everything you are responsible for; it means you are expected to be in front and providing guidance and direction to mitigate or enhance, depending on the item. It means you are, to a large degree, alone. Not lonely, but alone. Leadership is a solitary role that is accomplished with others.

Without the energy that can be derived from the well of energy that motivation provides, leadership would not be possible. Natural leaders have a natural connection to this well of energy. You see them simply bubbling over with energy and enthusiasm and it is simply fun to watch. It is especially fun to watch a leader who is energized and focused.

Principled Leadership;
A Balancing Act for a Lifetime

Those who are not natural leaders need to take some time and discover how they can access this energy to be able to sustain leadership, especially in the tough times. This is not easy. A person that does not have a natural well of energy and a spigot to connect with it must work hard not only to be the leader, but to find the means to find the energy to lead. This is more than twice as much work as the natural leader, but it can be done.

Leadership is so powerful and uplifting that it is exciting, powerful and energy filled! When you get that internal connection and align your motivation with your values in a desired direction – watch out! You will be so full of energy, passion and excitement that you will be awed at the experience!

Motivation is necessary as you pursue principled leadership. Energy is a constant need in order to be strong enough to do what needs to be done, especially in the long term activity of constantly seeking wisdom and gaining understanding throughout life.

Living principled leadership is a passion, and it has, at its core, motivation. But motivation is not an isolated process or a singular state of existence. Motivation comes from and rests upon another internal reality that we all share. That reality is the spirit with which we experience life.

- <u>Spirit</u>

Our spirit is a mystery. Our spirit dwells within us, yet at times it can seem so far away that it feels separate from us. Other times it feels like it is wholly who we are. As such, it has certain characteristics that are mystical and magical.

The mystery and magic of the spirit derives from the reality that it is in touch with the divine and is a reflection of our self in the divine scheme. Our spirit is our conduit to eternity. This is our only connection in this life to our most powerful and loving God. Because of this, learning about our spirit, working to understand it, striving to develop it; these are tasks each of us should undertake as a priority not only in our moments of need, but in our daily life. However, the spirit is the single biggest aspect of our lives that we ignore, and the most important item we must understand and embrace to find balance in our life.

We don't ignore our greed. We don't ignore our envy. We don't ignore our material needs. In fact, we use the first two to market the third. We have major corporations that thrive on finding better ways to use human characteristics to create motivational tools to sell products for one company over another. We have major corporations that thrive on finding better ways to influence attitudes and perspectives of people to get them to support certain political parties, political positions and politicians. All of these are material or human in nature, but not spiritual.

We have entertainment industries built on providing service to the flesh. We educate our children from pre-school through as much college as they can take, based on a misunderstood separation of church and state so we push God, and therefore spirit, out of education to prevent them from learning about morality and enlightened value. This creates a situation in which what is learned is again, material or human in nature, but not spiritual.

Yet we are creatures with two sides. We have a side that resides fully in the material world, and we have a side that does not. Our spirit is sometimes voiced by that secret inner person that is free from the constraints of the physical reality we live in, but we keep it uneducated and unused in our society. We do not do anything, except pray when things are tough, to reach out and embrace our spirit as part of our everyday life. Yet if we are to be whole, we must.

Establishing positive values require the individual to be a whole person. Being a whole person means to bridge the gap between the physical and spiritual aspects of life in order to create a whole and complete self. This is the primary reason principled leadership requires a connection through belief in God. Without the embrace of God, spirituality cannot exist; otherwise, what are you connecting with when you seek inner peace and enlightenment?

It is bringing the reality of our belief in God into our spirit that energizes it and brings it

Principled Leadership;
A Balancing Act for a Lifetime

to life to enable the full embrace of this aspect of self. Once our spirit is engaged, it provides the counterbalance needed to hold humanist ideas and desires at bay and provide balanced, consistent, value based, principled leadership.

I heard the analogy of an up/down relationship versus a side to side relationship as being the type of spiritual connection we need. For example, if you are connected with God, you have an up/down relationship that is singularly and spiritually strong. But if you have a side to side relationship you are more focused on what other people think about you, so your spirituality is less than your human needs.

The goal of developing and sustaining spirituality is to enable you to find the balance within. This gives you the leverage to fully utilize the motivation from inside to energize the value based characteristics of principled leadership, and provides consistency in the application of choice.

Principled Leadership;
A Balancing Act for a Lifetime

- <u>Conclusion</u>

These items then make up the additional items needed for specific pre-construction work as you seek to build principled leadership in your life. Courage, wisdom, virtue, value, motivation and spirit are items to grow and consider as you begin the active phase of construction and changing your life.

Balancing your life and the growth of principled leadership can only be achieved through selfless dedication to the goal of living rightly. Living rightly is, essentially, what personal leadership forces each of us to accomplish. This in turn, when strengthened, nourished and reinforced, is the foundation for living the best most effective life a human can live.

Chapter 3

Construction

The items in the previous chapters are not isolated or forgotten as you work to build your house. Instead, they are items that help you as you begin excavation work and construction. Now we begin talking about what it is you are building.

When I discussed building the home of your life, I mentioned several times the need to have the home built on the strongest possible foundation and made of the strongest possible values. I mentioned it needed to be strong, even unto death. Where can you find this type of building material?

The answer is quite simple, yet a stumbling block for many. Here is where my foundation is built, as it is solid and is, in my estimation, the very best foundation upon which to build.

Keep in mind; this is my personal journey, not the journey I believe everyone needs to travel to find the solution. We are all different and travelling different paths in different ways. But we all need to find a way to spiritual awareness.

• <u>Beginnings</u>

My father was a Methodist minister. As I remember, he had a lot of patience. As an example, when we lived in Adrian, Georgia, my best friend Gil and I let some crickets loose during church service one Sunday morning. Dad was in the pulpit and just looked at me, and said, "You boys get those crickets up and take them outside." He did not yell and was not angry. Even afterwards, he chuckled about it, but reinforced that the behavior we had demonstrated was not to be repeated, and it was not. It was also at this same church that I accepted Jesus Christ and was baptized when I was eleven years old. I grew up with the discussion, idea, values and praise of Christ around me. In the south, there was a rich tapestry of belief, and in my family, Jesus was center.

It wasn't so much that I actually did anything different because of my belief, it was that I behaved the way I did within the belief I held and grew from within it. For example, I have always believed that once you have accepted Christ in your life and honestly and openly asked for forgiveness of your sins, that you enter into a relationship that is beyond understanding or full explanation, because this relationship is one that takes you into the forever "now" of Jesus and puts you in His care. What is held by God cannot simply fall away and will not be tossed away. I believe the only way to withdraw from this relationship is to actively work at it and deny the Lord publicly and often. Even then, I am not sure if it happens.

So my life, the relationships, experiences, accomplishments, failures, shortcomings, learning's, marriages, children, partying, travels, you name it; that I have experienced are experienced from a perspective that God is the center and supreme. I have asked and He has forgiven me and loves me, and still forgives me for those things I still do that are sinful. (PS: This does not infer that I can do something I know is wrong and take the perceived forgiveness for granted up front – it does not work that way.) It makes Him more than a friend and more than a brother, counselor, coach, guide; it makes Him God and Father. It is an easy place, for me, to live, because I saw my family live within the relationship with Jesus every day.

I have discussed this perspective with many people and discovered that while many have, there are quite a lot of people that have not experienced this. Today, with God so marginalized in our society, perhaps a majority of people have no idea what it means to grow into a relationship with Him. They seem to believe that becoming a believer in Jesus Christ is the wrong path to take, because they see it as a limiting factor in their life and a marginal belief, rather than the unlimited spiritual experience that it actually is.

I found out one day that there was another layer to this relationship. While attending a small church in Ft. Walton Beach, Florida, I found myself sitting in a pew one Sunday evening, praying. A lot of life had happened since that day when I was eleven years old, and I felt the need to establish an adult, close relationship with Jesus that I knew I did not have at the time. I felt a need to take the burden and concerns of life and give them away. I felt a need for forgiveness for the things I had done wrong in life.

As I was sitting there praying, I discovered that I was in a very dark place. I think I could hear the congregation still singing, but I am not sure. I only can remember that I discovered I was in a pitch black space and I simply prayed to God to save me. I know the time for all of these events was moments, but to me, they seemed timeless. The first glimmer that something was happening was when I "saw" a tiny pin-prick of light suddenly appear. You know how you see the dust in the room when light shines in and you can see the shaft of light? Well that is exactly how I saw this tiny shaft of light.

Suddenly, another one appeared in a different place, and then another one, until I came to realize that these were holes in the mortar between the bricks that had my spirit walled up inside. These small holes began to expand and I could really see the brick pattern, when all of a sudden the entire wall collapsed and I was in a space of such brilliant white that it took my breath away. Suddenly, Jesus was there and I collapsed into His arms, safe, home, alive. I have never truly come up from that, and believe firmly that this encounter was with the living God.

Being so close to God, being loved unconditionally, being forgiven; there are no words that can truly explain the feeling these give to the spirit. I have no fear of what lays beyond death, because I believe firmly that I will be going home at that time, and transitioning into a permanent reality existence with God. What is there to fear?

This is the place where I have built my house – strong faith in God. This is the location to lay the foundation – on solid rock and not on sand; on consistent, proven, lasting principles.

In my Christian faith I believe that God sent His word to be tested in the physical form of Jesus Christ. He went through a very painful death, from being scourged thru being crucified. At no time did His principles, values or belief vary. He held strong, even through and beyond death. He showed us that the word of God is true, even unto death. Basing our own values and foundation on His strength is the surest means to find that strong foundation and structure that can last even unto death.

- <u>Values</u>

The result of my belief in the Lord is a desire to seek out and live the values that loving Jesus provides me. That does not mean to be religious. It means to live Christ like values – there is a difference. I cannot say that I am religious to any real degree. What I try to do is live the values I see in Christ. I don't always succeed in this, but I do want to and continuously work at it.

The values I therefore believe in and embrace are strong values, but as with anything in this life – they are only as strong as they can be as long as I remain focused on the values themselves. These values, displayed as virtues and known by words such as honesty, courtesy, respect, honor, equality, faith, belief, hope and love are the values that give energy and completeness. These are values that:

- Give hope in time of desolation,
- Give purpose in time of frustration,
- Give peace in time of despair, and,
- Bring me back when all is lost and there does not seem to be a way out.

These values are the building blocks of strength. These building blocks are not static, like stone; but are alive, powerful and dynamic. That is what makes these values so powerful, in that they give energy to the one who holds them close. Joining your personal character, initiative, motivation, activity, behavior and performance to values like honesty, equality and courtesy builds you into a person of value, both to yourself and to others.

Grounding yourself on these values provides a solid place to exist even when the world is at its most chaotic. But accomplishing that task is not easy and should not be viewed as something as simple as just making the choice. There is work to be done to get there. While we are born with the exposure of and ability to learn values, and we do learn them throughout our life, truly grasping the context of a value and embracing it, joining with it and empowering it in our life takes a lot more than being aware of it.

It takes time to build this house. Building this house starts with the foundation. It means excavating the dirt and laying the foundation in a way that will support the structure you desire to create. If you lay a foundation that is weak, the structure will collapse. But a strong foundation will support the structure and keep it secure for a lifetime. In the same way, to develop internal values you must excavate inside to lay a foundation inside that will support your values.

I remember when I was going through the toughest part of my life – deciding to get a divorce from my children's mother, that I had a fight. You see, I grew up in an environment where I simply expected that when two people "fell in love and got married" that they would be as happy together forever as my parents were. In this I was exceedingly naive.

But during the process of working through this I found myself in a yelling confrontation with God. Why could He do this to me? Why did I deserve this type of reality? Why did my kids have to experience this? How could He turn His back on me? The contest lasted several weeks.

Eventually, I came to terms with the choices I had to make. It took a little longer, but I realized that while I was yelling at God for my problems, He was actually carrying me through the tribulation I was experiencing.

This was one of the hardest excavating times of my life. I had to dig deep into the basic beliefs I had, the core of how I visualized, understood and interacted with life. I had to take a lot of misconceptions and naiveté out and understand the depth of the principles of faith I found. This enabled me to finally understand and grasp what true values are and how critical it is to embrace them fully.

That is why it is critical to come to a place in life where you can reach an understanding of the values that drive you. If you do not understand your own values, you do not have certainty that your foundation is strong, and your structure of values may quickly collapse when the storm comes – which will happen.

- <u>Faith & Belief</u>

This is the primary reason a strong value systems foundation must be faith and belief. I believe in Jesus Christ and have faith in Him. It is a singularity of power and strength that reduces all else to a shadow of concern. With this as the foundation, the structure has the best chance to succeed.

I am convinced that belief in God is essential in order to tame the beast within and force change on the inner person when that change is not necessarily liked or wanted. Taming one's self is both a difficult task and a necessary task and not one that is easily accomplished. Without a source of power and energy, most of us fail. Even with this source of power and energy we still falter and fall, but we can get back up with confidence and keep working at it. This is true of the big things and the little things in life.

Principled Leadership;
A Balancing Act for a Lifetime

I remember times when I failed in the character battle. There were times when the party life of my friends seemed to be so much fun and I wanted so much to be accepted by the group that I stepped over the line. These events put me in situations where I made choices that demonstrated my morality (which are values in action.) Many of these things I did, not because I really wanted to do them, but to fit in and be accepted by the group. It took a while, but I eventually learned that this was demonstrating a lack of conviction for the rightness of my choices. I simply had no power to control my own actions. I was lost in a life that I did not truly desire – I had no courage.

Belief in God provides power that is a critical fulcrum to use in the constant battle between the flesh and the spirit, because that is where the true measure of who we are is determined. Living simply for the flesh does not grow the whole person and will not yield principled leadership. Living in the spirit is not possible in this life, as we do reside in a fleshly body. So the place at which we need focus is at that point where the battle exists. The problem we all face is that without tools to use in fighting this battle, we fail to win it, causing our flesh to win more often than not – a situation that humanity has experienced since the very beginning of time and that will always exist in this physical world.

That is why the power of faith and belief are so important. This is the leverage we are offered to give us the strength to make good choices. This fulcrum enables us to leverage our belief in a way so as to prevent us, to a large degree, from doing things that we know we should not do and be able to have the strength to resist. Furthermore, having made the right choice, our belief becomes a well spring of power that reinforces our good decisions and helps us grow stronger in our character.

Don't misunderstand this to mean that by having faith or simply believing in God that you attain a state of near perfection, or that you reach a point where the battle between flesh and spirit suddenly ends. That state does not exist in this life. We all still fall down and have to get back up at times. But what this does accomplish is that it gives you the tools you can use to support your journey by attaining an attitude where you work at joining your existence to those values that yield positive, good results. It enhances your values as you live a value based life.

Here again is the province of wisdom, because a wise person can recognize how life changes and how we change within it and then have the courage to remain focused on the right way. That is why taking the time to understand and grow in wisdom teaches us the lessons we need to learn in order to remain focused for the long haul as we are living principled leadership.

• <u>Poor Foundation</u>

It is hard for me to grasp why anyone would not want access to the type of personal power these spiritual values provide. I think the major cause is that people are not aware of what is actually being offered. Our churches do not seem to be doing a very good job of educating people about how powerful our God is and how strong the principles and values of God are.

Principled Leadership;
A Balancing Act for a Lifetime

We appear to be failing in reaching out to people. Today the atheist suing believers and tradition gets the headlines. The standard of morality in the country is sliding and believers seem to be presented as people who are close to some throwback to a Neanderthal era and holding back progress to some unrecognizable perception of utopia.

But after you cut through to the chase, the only reason I believe that people do not seek this power is because of the things that must be given up in the process, versus what they perceive they gain through it. The things that must be giving up are physical reality centric things, like promiscuity, lust, greed, avarice, gluttony, drunkenness, lewdness, irreverence, and others; behaviors that are not behaviors that support positive growth toward solid core values. Our society provides a multitude of examples of these negative traits at work, always painted to be seen as good or normal behaviors.

Additionally, there are some who believe they do not need real values.

- There are some who say that God does not exist and that those of us who profess a belief are fools.

- There are some who say that all a person has to do is live in a good manner to live a good life without bringing "God" into it.

- There are some who say that believers in God set up a situation in which some people are winners and some are losers.

- There are some who say that because humans believe in a "God", people are killed and wars are fought.

The people who say these things perceive themselves to be enlightened and living in the real reality, but what they fail to grasp is that they are building a foundation that cannot last through death. Their foundation is weak and lacks wisdom.

- They depend only on their internal and very limited knowledge of their individual feeling and thinking.

- They deny the divinity and majesty of the universe.

- They deny the potential eternity that may exist.
- They detract from the love that exists within the hope of God and the ability to love others fully.
- They deny the reality of God alive and at work in heart, body, mind and spirit.
- They end up leaving the individual an empty shell without an ability to refill or seek another supportive energy source.
- They deny the reality of a spiritual interconnectedness.
- They deny spirit and only see that which is physical here and now.
- They do not believe in anything bigger than themselves, which is limiting in energy, spirit, hope, faith and all the attributes of virtue.

There are many reasons that non-believers have their perception of reality, and that is ok. We are a people made up of many parts and I wish them well. However, reality is not a place that only non-believers can see. Reality is a set of circumstances that enable an individual to grasp understanding and weave place, purpose, texture, spirit and context into a perception of that reality. These are not circumstances that any single individual can grasp in isolation from wisdom, and wisdom cannot be grasped without fully integrating the physical reality with the spiritual reality into a blended, worshipful aspect of divinity around us.

This is not to say that people who do not have a belief in God cannot develop leadership, of course they can. But it is a significant limiting factor in their ability to establish principled leadership.

The singular item that is not said enough is about what is gained through faith and belief. Things like peace, patience, less stress, certainty of eternal life. The marketplace does not hear about the hope that is found through God's love, or the unconditional love we are embraced with. These need to be out there as a counter-point to the negativity.

Principled Leadership;
A Balancing Act for a Lifetime

- <u>Spirituality</u>

In the previous section I mentioned that it is hard for me to grasp why anyone would not want access to the type of personal power these spiritual values provide. The question many will ask is simply this: what kind of power?

The power of the spirit is not the power of Darth Vader or Yoda in *Star Wars*. I am not talking about an ability to hold rocks in the air or sweep the floor without touching the broom. The power of the spirit is stronger than that.

The spirit is connected via an undetectable thread of energy directly into the energy of God. In essence, this makes our spirit part of God. Through this connection we can establish a connection with others spirits.

When people pray together, they are focusing this energy in a single direction and the synergy that is gained is huge. The power of prayer is real, if only felt at times in the spirit and not the body of the one receiving the prayer.

A key failure of our society is a failure to respect and embrace this power of the spirit. Instead we focus to a fault on technology and personal liberty and how we can manipulate or control the physical reality. We are missing so much.

The spirit is mysterious. How we can be one with it, walk through the portal of reality with it, experience things the body cannot understand through it, and come alive in a complete manner because of it, is all a mystery.

The power of spirit gives you the power to leverage God's love and help build strength of character. The power of spirit enables a person to truly live principled leadership.

- <u>Challenges</u>

As stated earlier, it is on the inside that the hard work of building and embracing values takes place. It is on the inside where the energy must be found to understand, embrace and live the values that are spiritually based and found through a personal relationship with God. It is on the inside where we live.

Our physical senses are our windows that we have to observe and interact with the world on the outside. These are the windows we use to see out, but these are also the windows the world uses to penetrate inside. It is in the control of these windows that the first statement of the internal value commitment is made.

When filth, crime, murder, unfaithfulness, lawlessness, pain and drama are pervasive on the television, internet, and music and in movies, the choice must be made internally as to what level of exposure to allow. It is a critical and highly difficult question, because it involves the internal decision to embrace something different than what is portrayed as the norm in our society. The biggest problem with this is that most people want to be seen as normal by their peers, even though they want to be independent or unique at the same time. Adapting an attitude that says the norms of society as displayed through the entertainment and news media of our day are not your own norms takes courage.

This is especially true in the development of internal values, as courage is an internal value. It takes courage to separate from the crowd. It takes courage to establish control over your desires and wants. It takes courage to stop doing those things your body wants to do because they feel so good, and do those things your spirit says do because they are the right things to do.

Reaching a place in life where you realize that you simply cannot do it alone is the place where you begin the search for truth. Searching for truth can only lead to God, as He is the arbiter of truth. Having sought and found God in your life, you now have a strong ally to help as you begin the work of laying your foundation, and then to begin building values on that foundation through your choices, actions and attitude.

It is simply a wonderful experience to be honest with yourself and with others, and not have to lie about what you are doing or why you are making your choices. It is freedom in the purest sense of the word, because you do not have a cloud of doubt hanging over you.

It is simply wonderful to embrace the goodness that exists once the ugliness is shut out. There is good in everyone, but sometimes, when we allow ourselves to be negatively focused because we are deep into the 24/7 news cycle, negative news reporting, bias, anger, drama and vulgarity on television, music, movies, etc., we forget to be positive. This is one of the primary benefits of growing values within, in that you have the opportunity to turn the negativity off and embrace the positive.

- <u>Impact</u>

I have heard some people say that what we see and hear does not affect us, because as adults, we are able to choose between embracing them and rejecting them. While I understand the intellectual intent of that comment, it is simply not true. We are what we listen to and see, because information enters our window and touches our inner self and ultimately becomes an integral part of who we are through affecting our experience, which ultimately shapes our internal tools for evaluating whether something is actually good or bad.

The things we see on television, movies, internet, at clubs, parties, and any other place; the things we hear in these same places and our music; the things we read; all of these influence who we are. This influence of who we are is the influence of who we become. You cannot separate what enters your person from the person. To say otherwise is self delusion and deception. It is like saying you can get a little pregnant but not be pregnant. The truth is, either you are pregnant or you are not. There is no middle ground.

Yet we continue to delude ourselves that somehow, we are isolated and unique individuals who are unaffected by any aspect of life around us. An interesting argument I heard recently went along these lines:

- We ask ourselves, is this right or wrong? We kid ourselves into believing there is a very fine line between the two.

- So we move closer to the line and we ask ourselves, is this still right or wrong? We then tell ourselves that it is mostly right and only hints at the idea of being wrong, so we justify our position.

- Then we move a little further and we justify the new position by saying that while it may not be right, our intention is good, so it is ok. In reality, we have stepped over the line.

In this we perform the very work Jesus talked about, when he talked about the hypocrites, the Pharisee's, in behaviors He discussed in Matthew Chapter 23, verses 23 and 24. These verses say, *"Woe to you, teachers of the law and Pharisees, you hypocrites! You give a tenth of your spices—mint, dill and cummin. But you have neglected the more important matters of the law—justice, mercy and faithfulness. You should have practiced the latter, without neglecting the former. You blind guides! You strain out a gnat but swallow a camel."*

We are straining to find justification for the things we do wrong, instead of simply not doing wrong. Part of this justification today involves saying that the things we are exposed to and generating in our society do not negatively impact us. It is another way of not holding ourselves accountable for the action of generating those things that are wrong, which includes the high level of filth in our entertainment. After all, if that filth does not harm us, well, what's the harm? Having television with filth on 24 hours a day does not mean kids will see it, so no harm. However, adults see it. We are all harmed by filth, as it degrades respect for the other individuals and groups of people within our society.

So in this we have not changed, we are still hypocrites. The only way to break out of that is to go through the earnest task of finding God, building the foundation that only He can offer, embracing the values that He provides, and living those values in everyday life.

It is as easy as a simple choice. It is as difficult as moving a mountain. It all depends on how you try and do it. Embrace God; it is a simple choice, although still hard work. Do not embrace God; it is impossible regardless of the amount of work you go through.

The beginning point, the simple choice that many people stumble over, is the simple choice to seek and then accept God. It is a necessary step in the growth process. It makes everything else make sense.

Principled Leadership;
A Balancing Act for a Lifetime

- Building Strong Values

Reaching this point in life is the beginning of establishing the internal values I mentioned earlier; honesty, courtesy, respect, honor, equality, faith, belief, hope and love. This is only the starting point, as building the structure of values on your foundation of belief is a life time opportunity and challenge.

Take any one of these and you can see the effort required and the reward provided. For example, equality requires the development of the attitude that all are equal before God. When you truly believe that, you cannot discriminate or be prejudiced against someone simply because they are different. It is a very difficult value to embrace, but it is critical in establishing place. What I mean by place is that we have only one God, and all of us are equal in His sight. Therefore to believe or behave in a way that says your neighbor is inferior to you because they are different from you, is not establishing your place at the throne of God, because you deny others the equality they have from God.

Principled Leadership;
A Balancing Act for a Lifetime

Once you have laid the foundation and built your structure you will be required to provide maintenance to it for your entire life. This is rewarding, time consuming and hard work. Sometimes, you have to go all the way back to the foundation and re-pour it and build it all over again. If you could stay internal all the time, this might not be so difficult, but the truth is, we live in this world, and living in this world our values interact with those around us to find the place where we fit the best.

People do evaluate you and yes, they will judge you based upon their observation. It is important, therefore, to think about what people are seeing in you when they observe you. It is also important to understand that as a believer in God, people will be evaluating God who lives in you as well as yourself, so it becomes important to understand what you are projecting into the world for all to see.

Wisdom is the first fruit of the application of courage in directing your life. Wisdom is the critical bridge that takes you from a place where you are living this life, to a place where you live a full life. The fruit of wisdom, virtue, is the foundation of life and the demonstration of your values in life. Without virtue, we are only living life to reproduce and die. Virtue demonstrates wisdom. Wisdom means you are celebrating the divine nature of God.

- Growth

We grow our internal values into pillars of strength through the testing of life. Life, as they say, happens. We learn, fail, stand up, fall down, get back up and somewhere in the midst of living, our values are tested by real life. This testing we all experience either reinforces our values or knocks them over. The good thing about knocked over values is that God never turns His back on us, so we need to get back up and rebuild our values and do better the next time. The other thing about knocked over values is that perhaps we discover that our values were not built on the right foundation. Maybe destroyed values mean it's time to look deeper into Gods plan and love for us to lead us to the right values where the right foundation can be laid.

Principled Leadership;
A Balancing Act for a Lifetime

It is a continuous and great cycle that is best described as living principled leadership. As we age, maybe we don't have so many ups and downs, or maybe we do. How we live through life, the wisdom we gain, the courage we possess and how our values form becomes the critical measure of our life. If we adapt an aura of bitterness because we are not getting what we believe we are owed in this life, then we are truly failing to grasp the love of God in our heart. If we adapt the love of God in our heart, we recognize that we are not owed anything by anyone in life, and accept the gift of what is given with reverence and thankfulness.

Many people seem to behave as if they are living in a dress rehearsal of life, but not really participating in life. Living as if the current event is a dress rehearsal takes away the gravity of even the smallest choices made, and demonstrates a lack of awareness and value. Embracing values means you are here, now, living every moment because you are thankful of the moment and give each moment value. People who do these things clearly demonstrate a set of values that exists on the inside and project those values through the life they lead by the way they interact with it.

As part of our continuous creation and reinforcement of our internal values we project them into the world for others to see. As we project these values into the world, we demonstrate a certain type of behavior that enables those around us to evaluate our value system and find a way to interact with us.

Many people use a different word than evaluate; they refer to judgment of people. It is true that in Matthew 7, verse 1, Jesus said, *"Judge not, that ye be not judged."* However, the reality is that all of us evaluate people by making a discriminatory choice that does not involve the worth or value of the person. These evaluations are how we become friends with some people and not with others and other similar choices. Not being friends with a person is not a judgment of that person. Instead, it is a choice of comfort.

Judgment is different. Judgment is the determination of a person's worth. In this, judging someone can be harsh and cruel.

Principled Leadership;
A Balancing Act for a Lifetime

Yet, when you live a life of value, you inevitably run up against those who would judge you as unworthy, simply because that is what they believe to be appropriate. After all, as I mentioned earlier, to some you are holding back progress by hanging onto ancient, irrational beliefs. In these cases, your value system is challenged, and your foundation may be shaken. However, these are the times when you maintain your belief and stay strong; and the reward in spirit is high.

Having taken the time to construct your house through the development of your internal values through your belief in God, it is time now to "move in" to your house and begin to show others your work.

Chapter 4

Post-Construction

Up to now we have discussed your decision on where to build, what materials to use and worked through the expectations for completion of the construction phase of your house. You should, by now, have established a strong spiritual center in your life and are beginning to grow in those values that reflect this change. You are now working on balancing the physical with the spiritual and establishing a clear strong structure from which to live. I understand that completing these items can be a lifelong quest all by themselves, yet these are things you must do in order to move forward towards principled leadership.

In many ways, what you have been working on and are still working on is the biggest change in your life – providing a balancing act to create yourself as a whole person. It also is probably the hardest part of this process – changing your core values. Yet it is the most rewarding as well, gaining you wisdom, energy, passion, virtue in life, and teaching you that love overcomes all. All of this has been mostly internal activity.

In the next phase we shift more in the direction of external activity, although all that you are and do in sustaining balance and embracing principled leadership rests on the internal foundation of belief and faith. In this post-construction phase you are furnishing your house, planting your garden, having an open house and then living in your house, so to speak.

This is when people begin to see the fruit of your labor. This is where the values you have created and embraced are revealed to others. This is where you meet the conflicts of the world and where your values, your house, gets rattled by the elements that oppose it. Let's begin by talking about those attributes that others should see in you.

- Fruit

There are many behaviors that arise from the embrace of your developing value system.

Principled Leadership;
A Balancing Act for a Lifetime

Here are a few of the fruit that should demonstrate that you are truly grounded spiritually and living the values of personal integrity and character. We turn our attention to Jesus and his sayings.

- <u>Selfless.</u> Jesus said, in Matthew 7, verse 12: *"Therefore, whatever you want men to do to you, do also to them, for this is the Law and the Prophets."* Living life based on positive values is not conducive to being selfish, because being selfish prevents you from giving of yourself by doing things for others. Doing things for others is self-rewarding. While it is hopefully returned by others in like manner, the initial step, doing things for others, requires selflessness in order to take that step without the realization or expectation of a reward for the action. It is not a quid quo pro, in that by doing something for someone else you will always get like returned. Instead, it is a behavior of selflessness you demonstrate because it is the right thing to do on its own merits. This is why it is visible evidence through external behavior that reflects the values existing on the inside.

- <u>Positive.</u> Jesus said, in Matthew 5, verse 3, *"Blessed are the poor in spirit, for theirs is the kingdom of heaven."* Pride harms people. Embracing the attitude of being poor in spirit forces one to swallow pride and put it aside. Being prideful or negative deprives those around you of the energy necessary to be productive, upbeat, or joyous. A positive, respectful and reverent attitude demonstrates the peace within, the hope that resides in your heart and the determination to be thankful and gracious for the gifts received. Being positive is yet another way to value people, in that you choose to find the positive around you and the positive within them, which shows your respect for others and your desire to provide them your good energy.

- <u>Respectful.</u> Jesus said, in Matthew 5, verse 4, *"Blessed are those who mourn, for they will be comforted."* To show people you respect them gives them of yourself, because it elevates them and evens the field between you. Showing respect for others shows that you understand the power of respect, which comes from respect for God first, and self second. Respecting others enables you to mourn their loss, even while celebrating their life. Joining with others through respect builds strength and strong relationships.

- Reverent. Jesus said, in Matthew 5, verse 5, *"Blessed are the meek, for they will inherit the Earth."* We reverence not only our God, but also the life that we are given. To embrace an attitude of reverence means we behave in a way that is respectful of others, that supports, holds fast to love, is there for our friends and family, believes in God, respects His creation and recognizes, at the end of the day, that we are given a unique gift – the gift of life; and an even greater gift – the gift of free spirit. We accept these gifts and recognize the greatness of our God. This recognition of our place leads us to be meek in ourselves as we lower the value we find in our own knowledge and understanding and worth, while grasping the greatness of God. God could have created us without the ability to choose to love Him, but He did not. Instead, we each are born with the ability to choose what we believe in, within the limits of what we learn growing up and the influences around us. This special gift of life and choice is so much more valuable than many seem to believe. This is the very best of a truly loving Father, who wants so much to give us the universe, but lets us choose for ourselves. Loving God as a friend means being willing to lay down our life for Him. This is a place in our spirit to feel the intensity of faith and hold still in reverence of the love He has for us and the gifts He has given us.

- <u>Fair.</u> Jesus said, in Matthew 5, verse 6, *"Blessed are those who hunger and thirst for righteousness, for they will be filled."* Fairness is an application of conscious choice that reflects the behavior of being fair and seeking the rightness of choice. It shows people that you truly care about them. It gives people assurance that you will not rush to judgment, but take the time to evaluate all of the information to reach the right conclusion. It shows that you do not discriminate or act with prejudice, because you take the time to control you inner choices. It clearly demonstrates that you exist on the bedrock of the right kind of values.

- Supportive. Jesus said, in Matthew 5, verse 7, *"Blessed are the merciful, for they will be shown mercy."* Being supportive demonstrates value because it provides value of others to them. When you support people, you show you care, you demonstrate that their very being is important to you. Showing people you care about them through your action gives them mercy by enabling them to not be judged by you or looked at harshly. Supporting people is having mercy on them, because it is in a sense both loss and harshness, or unmerciful, to be treated in a way that is unsupportive.

Principled Leadership;
A Balancing Act for a Lifetime

- <u>Honest.</u> Jesus said, in Matthew 5, verse 8, *"Blessed are the pure in heart, for they will see God."* Honesty begins inside and is a true form of purity. If you are not honest with yourself, you certainly cannot be honest with others. It is not difficult to evaluate someone's behavior in this area, because the truth is oftentimes readily available, so someone's words are testable. It is critical as a behavior to be honest, so you build credibility and earn respect because your behavior demonstrates the values that you believe in and show that you can be believed. This honest behavior defines the pure heart that lives within.

- <u>Peaceful.</u> Jesus said, in Matthew 5, verse 9, *"Blessed are the peacemakers, for they will be called Sons of God."* Being peaceful does not mean a person does not experience stress. As humans, we experience stress, and it is both good and bad. However, being peaceful is a behavior of finding compromise, not pointing fingers, not creating stress where none exists, and not stirring things up simply because you can. Being peaceful has a lot to do with being a peacemaker. Being peaceful represents the value inside and the foundation of life – which equates to the end state of grace and eternity. Behaving in a peaceful manner then, reflects the internal value of being peaceful. Behaving peacefully means to not be quick to anger, lose your patience or express negativity.

- <u>Courageous.</u> Jesus said, in Matthew 5, verse 10, "*Blessed are those who are persecuted because of righteousness, for theirs is the kingdom of heaven.*" Part of being courageous is demonstrating a willingness to say what needs to be said. Many people fear saying something they believe would place them in a position to lose status, friends or respect. Truthfully, being courageous should not cause these things when done in the spirit of love that all of these behavior characteristics demonstrate. Even so, sometimes it takes courage to be the one to say what needs to be said to someone that needs to hear it.

- <u>Friendly.</u> Jesus said in John Chapter 15, verse 13, *"Greater love has no one than this, that he lay down his life for his friends."* Friends are people in our life that we care about. With these individuals, we establish a friendly attitude and perspective. In order to have friends, we are friendly. In order to be friendly, we find that value of friendship inside and embrace it. Ultimately, the value of being friendly is that it helps generate positive energy and encourage people around us. It shows, yet again, that we value the people we are being friendly towards. This is a clear indication of someone who is behaving based upon a good value. Do they have good friends with good values, or do they have friends in name only or who behave in bad ways?

As you can see, all of these are linked into a cohesive vision of someone who has a solid value system founded on a belief in God and respect for Him. How else can life be established so as to be an effective life? What else can be so important that it detracts from the central, core process of finding and establishing these values inside?

• <u>Challenges</u>

Perception is a dangerous thing, because perception is reality. People draw conclusions about you based upon their reality that is based on their perceptions, so it is critical to be aware of this.

The message from Jesus is to have faith and believe. Having faith and believing in Him brings out certain value characteristics. Living those characteristics has texture and substance. Living in this manner creates the causation for a certain behavior, which yields a tangible result in the world we live in. This tangible result is the basis for the value system we demonstrate through our behavior.

But the world we live in works at holding us back and keeping us down. The temptations to fail are so numerous that it would take many more books than this to list them all. These human centric things I mentioned before, like promiscuity, lust, greed, gluttony, drunkenness and irreverence, are constant companions in the life we lead because they manifest from the flesh we are part of and seek to bring us down and hold us at that level.

As I mentioned, this is where the battle truly exists. Living in your values (house) you will be constantly buffeted by the winds of these negative behaviors, as well as others. Your faith will be challenged. Your perseverance will be challenged, but with wisdom will eventually become your friend. To use the analogy:

- You will get termites in your walls,
  - Until you learn how to keep them away.
- You will have weeds in your yard,
  - Until you learn to treat for them regularly before they appear.
- Your sink will slowly drain,
  - Until you learn how to clean it properly.
- Your garden will not grow very well,
  - Until you learn to water and fertilizer it appropriately.

Principled Leadership;
A Balancing Act for a Lifetime

I hope you get the idea, that just as with a home, your values will be challenged, until you learn to keep focused on the values themselves, have faith and believe. That takes courageous living and revelation that comes from wisdom gained; all of which comes from the love of God.

- Conclusion

The fruit of your life is the virtue you show in life. This is created through living your life based on positive values that are tempered through wisdom and lived courageously. This is the journey, not simply to attain this state of existence, but to sustain it. In essence, this is the path that must always be walked, because staying on the path is maintaining balance and living principled leadership.

In describing this process of living principled leadership, I said it was a cycle and that each of us joins at the place where we are now. This is true and continues to all phases of our life, as the evaluation and strengthening of our foundation and structure, and living our values, never ends.

Principled Leadership;
A Balancing Act for a Lifetime

We will shift out of the analogy now and discuss living in the value systems of the world around us. All of the steps we have discussed to this point must be alive within you at all times. Through the various phases of building the "house," you should now be in a position to understand the amount of work to be done to get to this point and to sustain it for a lifetime.

Since the goal is to live a life of principled leadership, it must be a leadership that can last through the onslaught of life. The process up to this point has been to build the internal foundation that provides the strength to continue the journey into the world around and succeed, as well as what people should be able to see as you live a principled life and bear fruit.

The remaining discussion shifts fully to the external interaction in the world we live in, and discuss how we can effectively continue reinforcing and sustaining principled leadership throughout our life.

Chapter 5

Sharing Value Systems

- Getting Started

The first phase for sharing value systems is to understand your own value system. By now, you should have worked through the process of self exploration and discovery; conducted some serious analysis and review; made decisions about your values and who you truly are and want to become; and worked through to a point where you are now living the positive values we have discussed – which is your value system.

The next phase is to transition into a relationship with others based upon shared value systems, as the foundation of our relationships within our society and our species is based on the aspects of our value systems that we have in common, or share.

How you do this is critical to your on-going growth and a continuation of all that we have discussed. Being true to your developed value system while interacting with others value systems will be challenging. There are many people you will meet who share so many commonalities with you that you need feel no need to energize yourself to defend your values. With these individuals, often members of your family or close friends, you share a very similar value system. But the further away from your family and close friends you go, and especially the further away from those people who live positive God inspired values you go, the more you will discover the variance in value systems.

We share a host of values. We share values in our towns, cities, states, regions, country and world. We share certain values with our co-workers and with the people we hang out with. In most cases these value systems overlap sufficiently to allow us to live with a certain level of expectation of the general behavior we can expect, and that others can expect from us.

In travelling around the world, I discovered that our value systems are inclusive enough and overlapping enough to include people from other countries and religions, because we share some basic values simply as human beings living life, having kids, raising families, worrying about the bills, providing for our families, making life safe and being there for each other.

- <u>Challenges & Similarities</u>

But there are challenges as well. As an example, as American citizens we value citizenship and have a set of behaviors and actions derived around how we treat citizens versus non-citizens. It is not as simple as saying the law denies access or requires punishment for non-citizens. Our shared value system is larger than that and goes to the belief that as citizens we are endowed with certain inalienable rights and privilege that non-citizens can never have. We value our citizenship and share that as a mutual binding tie between us.

When our citizenship appears to lose value we all feel a sense of devaluation and loss. Over the past several years we have all observed the apparent unlimited entry of illegal immigrants (not to be confused with legal immigration which we almost all accept) into our country and the war of words between our politicians. However, the inability of those political leaders to simply enforce the law and stop the inflow of illegal immigrants devalues our own citizenship. This is a mutual value that we all share as part of our mutual value system and has meaning for us.

Some of the pieces of our value systems can be quite innocent. For example, the reason we say please and thank you is not simply because it is courteous, but because our value system may include courtesy within it. This is a shared value many of us have. When someone says thank you for a courteous act, like opening a door, we are rewarded and feel we did the right thing. This feeds our value system and reinforces that system, and brings those involved closer together.

Contrarily, when we hold the door for someone and they simply walk through and don't acknowledge the courteous thing we did, we may feel hurt, confused or irritated, because that other person did two things: 1) they did not validate our value system and 2) they demonstrated they are participants in a different value system from our own and directly, even if unconsciously, devalued our value system. This is seen as rude behavior by the holders of the courtesy value system, but as normal behavior by those who do not share this value system.

It is interesting that even something as minor as a failure of courtesy can create friction between people. Imagine then how a big value system conflict generates friction that leads to war between people.

Looked at another way, some of the pieces of our value system are tough. For example, for someone who values life in all its forms and fallacies all the way through natural death, the thought of someone being executed for murder or any other reason is horrendous. Not only is this individual's value system not validated when someone is executed; and not only is the process of execution demonstrating the government, law or political process is in a different value system from their own; but their sense of outrage comes from the singular choice the system makes which appears to be directly challenging their value system. It is not simply a case where the government unconsciously or indirectly devalues the holder's value system – in this case it is perceived from the holder of this value that the government and the majority of the people of the country purposefully devalue their value system, which fills this with energy and makes it powerful for them.

- Shared

There are many people who share a common value system.

- Bikers share an appreciation for the open road and even the noise of their machines.
- Gymnasts share an appreciation of physical strength and form.
- Ballet dancers share an appreciation for power, form and grace.
- Chefs share an appreciation for creativity and consistency and the ability to deliver excellence in the meals they prepare.
- Gangs share an appreciation for power and strength focused on control of

others with the use of intimidation and violence.

In short, groups share certain values that are inherently part of that group. In this case, the value systems of the individuals adopt these values as their own and become part of the larger value system of the group, even while they share these values with only certain other people who also share this value. By the same token, value systems can clash. The value system of believers in God and of gangs, for example, significantly clash.

Value systems are complex. You can share in a value system that is highly rigid or excessively loose, or anywhere in between. Value systems are dictated from within the system itself, not necessarily applied from an external force; although many values are learned through the auspices of external origin. Even as children we learn values through the interaction with and observation of our parents, other adults, peers, teachers, etc. But the acceptance and application of a value within one's own personal value system is an internal choice, not an external causation.

Principled Leadership;
A Balancing Act for a Lifetime

When I joined the US Air Force in 1973, I was a long haired high school graduate, basically living the lifestyle of a carefree youth. The value system I went into was far different from the one I left, but there were also many similarities, such as respect, trust and belief in country. In this case the people already in the USAF, drill instructors and others, took us and built upon the shared pieces of our value systems to create within us a new layer value system that valued the things military service provided. Things like duty and honor, which are values in many people, are stronger, in general, for those serving in the military.

- Culture

There are many value systems within our culture, as our culture is made up of all the value systems we share. These are values that the vast majority of people share everywhere on our planet. It is these shared values that bind us together. These values, when added to each nation's unique history, declarations, constitutions or ideologies make up these different and unique nations. But many of the values are similar.

- We share the value of fairness.
    - o Nearly all of us share the value that decisions and actions should be fair.
    - o We believe people should be treated fairly simply because we also want to be treated fairly.
- We share the value of honesty.
    - o Nearly all of us share a value that spoken and written words from people should be honest and not deceitful.
    - o We believe we should be honest with others because we expect others to be honest with us.
- We share a value of competency.
    - o Nearly all of us share a value that people should be competent at their work.
    - o We believe people should be competent in the work they perform for us and that we should be competent at the work we perform for others.

- o Competency is a value that is seldom mentioned but that is an inherent part of nearly all of our value systems.
- We share a value of respect.
  - o Nearly all of us share a value that individuals deserve respect, because we also want respect.
  - o Respect for our person, our property and our rights are fairly well established within most of our value systems.
- We share the value of personal responsibility.
  - o Nearly all of us believe we are responsible for our fate.
  - o However, the gap in this value is widening as more and more people seem to share a value that they are victims rather than responsible individuals. But still, the vast majority accepts this as a mutual value.

These are not the only values people share, in general terms, between most value systems and most of the people, but it provides a foundation to grasp that people in nearly every category share certain values to one extent or another. These shared values are the glue that binds people together in the life of a family, society, culture and nation. These are the values that provide people with commonality of experience and expectation that enables a group, as a people, to move forward in a cohesive, organized and unified manner.

These shared aspects of value systems are what make for and sustains a united people. Divergent value systems are basically an aberration to this process. For example, polygamists who have multiple children with multiple wives are not in the value system of many countries, while they are in others. Whether or not that was a value to the people thousands of years ago or in other places and times on our planet, they are not values Americans share in our common value system today.

- People who sell illegal drugs are not considered to be part of our value system, as we value the rule of law and these people are outside of that.

- Terrorism, gang behavior or any behavior that harms innocent people or children is outside of our basic value system.

- Abuse by people who are in a position of great personal trust is well outside of our value system.

- Greed and excessive income by people perceived as profiting off of the pain of the people is outside our value system. However, we value wealth and the hard work it takes to earn it. We value the idea that someone should be able, through their own hard work, to raise themselves up and become wealthy.

America is a diverse and complex culture that exists in relationship with multiple cultures around the world. Even as we can identify our value systems, we know that they are constantly changing. Each generation modifies the meaning and understanding of the values we utilize for our value system.

Principled Leadership;
A Balancing Act for a Lifetime

- <u>Danger</u>

However, there are some values that have remained consistent over time and these are the very basic positive values we discussed through the first few chapters of this book. As an example, the value of being honest is unchanging. Either you are being honest or you are not. Truth does not change. We cannot therefore say we are changing the value of honesty. In essence, to change the meaning or value of honesty means to be dishonest.

The example being set by our political leadership is such that honesty appears to be a vague concept. The ability for someone to stand up and say X, when X is clearly not the truth, and not be challenged by anyone except the opposition, shows that honesty is not necessarily valued.

The onslaught of verbiage and example in the press reflects that our overall leadership does not value the simplicity honesty provides. But of greater impact, this behavior appears to attempt to undermine a basic value and will have far reaching negative consequences.

Principled Leadership;
A Balancing Act for a Lifetime

Quite simply, the danger we face is that as with the value of honesty above, as people behave in a manner so as to make changes to the understanding of or value of basic values, these values lose their power. However, these very foundational cohesion points are the glue that binds us together and without that glue, we could fragment.

Value systems are very large encompassing structures that give us context and help us manage our expectations as we move through time. Without shared values within value systems, individuals do not have anything to relate to each other with, no context or purpose. Essentially, when no one shares values or has reason to become associated with any group, anarchy prevails.

Value systems then, in this context, keep us from fragmenting by giving us enough commonality to remain united in the face of adversity or disaster. Our value systems then are part of our national identity and our national treasure. If we tinker with them, we run the risk of undermining the very fabric of our nation.

Principled Leadership;
A Balancing Act for a Lifetime

Leadership application, either from within each person or within the group as a whole, is the central point where activity takes place that directly affects how we understand and feel about our shared values and which values are the strength of the society at a given time. This is powerful, and is one of the primary motivations for this book, because if we disconnect ourselves from a common value system, or if we fail to create effective positive values for those systems, we lead ourselves blindly and we fall.

It is the shared and common values of our society that we must actively reinforce if our value systems are to survive and hold us together. This is a driving force for principled leadership – strengthening our values and therefore our value systems.

The work starts at the personal level and expands outward. As you interact with the values others have, you contact their value system. How you interact tells who you are, but it also tells you who they are. More importantly, this contact gives you the opportunity to influence their value system.

Principled Leadership;
A Balancing Act for a Lifetime

In your day to day contact with people then, consciously think and actively pursue a positive influence on people's value systems. When the majority of people positively influence value systems, the overall values of the group improve. Improving the value systems of the group can only lead to a stronger and more cohesive group. This is the impact of positive principled leadership.

- <u>Live the Example</u>

Our values demonstrate the positive aspect of principled leadership. God inspired values give positive energy and power to those who hold them close and live them daily.

In Matthew, chapter 5 verses 14-15, Jesus said, *"14 "You are the light of the world. A town built on a hill cannot be hidden. 15 Neither do people light a lamp and put it under a bowl. Instead they put it on its stand, and it gives light to everyone in the house."*

Living these God inspired values is the power to be that light on the hill. Believers need to demonstrate the positive values Jesus has shown us, and allow those around us to see the truth of the power of Christ in our lives.

How are we demonstrating our God inspired values when we call our fellow Americans vile names, or when we lose our patience with a co-worker or family member over something that is, in essence, insignificant? Are we demonstrating these values when we judge our neighbor because of the political party they affiliate with? Are we demonstrating our faith and belief in God when we condemn one religion but support another? What about if we are needlessly or purposefully noisy and disturb our neighbors? Living these values is an all-the-time activity, not something we only do when we go to church.

While those who believe in God should not walk around with a prideful air, we should feel comfort in knowing we are demonstrating Christ in us for those around us through our behavior. We are being the light on the hill.

So it is critical to be aware of your behavior when you are living within your value system and interacting with others. There will be conflicts and misunderstandings. There will be times when it seems you are communicating with someone from another planet, simply because you can't find anything in common to work with.

But usually, you will discover that you easily find a way to work through situations that arise in an effective manner. After all, a positive value system contains courtesy, empathy, honesty, support, fairness, respect, and a host of other positive characteristics that should provide you with the patience necessary to gain understanding. The other person or group may not have these and it could be trying; but have faith and believe, and you will persevere.

- <u>Conclusion</u>

This stage of life then is for establishing and living principled leadership. It is one thing to work on the internals of developing character; but it is quite another to operate in the world at large and not fall away from those values. It is yet another step to actively portray the values of positive principled leadership as a counter-point to the negative values or value destroying behavior around us. It is a final step to live God given values daily in all aspects of life and be evidence of how good, positive and powerful God's values are.

This is where courage, wisdom and motivation come into play. This is where you are confronted by choices that are very difficult to manage, but that must be made. This is where your faith and belief in God is tested and fulfilled every day.

Chapter 6

Living Principled Leadership

Living principled leadership is the greatest and final challenge life offers. At the end of the day, to be able to look in the mirror and in good conscience know you have done all you could do in every situation in the right way for the right reasons is the final test. Facing yourself with honesty is the closest you get, on this side of the wall of reality, to facing your creator.

The power this type of moment has in life is that in this moment your conscience is bearing witness to your actions. The power of the conscience cannot be understated. However, this is also one last place where the drive to live a balanced life and principled leadership is under attack in our culture.

- Conscience

Conscience is that determinant that cries out inside as to the rightness or wrongness of the decisions taken or the words spoken in all aspects of our lives. In essence, it is the last guide available that enables a clear and correct choice in a situation that is complex, compelling or confusing.

Paul said, in Romans, Chapter 2, verse 15: *"They show that the requirements of the law are written on their hearts, their consciences also bearing witness, and their thoughts sometimes accusing them and at other times even defending them."* Clearly, the conscience is that which helps us decide the rightness or wrongness of our actions.

The biggest effort on the part of some in our culture today appears to be action designed to downgrade the reliance on or the referral to the conscience in regards to the choices people make. This is done primarily through the auspices of the connection with Jesus to conscience as an "out of date experience;" and done through the constant onslaught of information, entertainment, a barrage of news and misinformation and activity that is slanted in such a way as to demonstrate that it is ok not to believe. These also prevent people from having the quiet time needed to reflect on actions and words to find a semblance of guidance on the rightness of those actions and words.

Pushing to remove references to God out of our society in almost any context degrades the value people place in the conscience. Upping the relevancy of rationalization degrades the value of conscience. These are on-going activities that are fully underway in our society and assist in reducing the value of the conscience in our lives, because the conscience needs the balanced life that only the spirit alive within can provide.

The removal of guilt for action based upon the reduction in the value of conscience is a valid process to those who rationalize that human value is the apex in the pursuit of success or power. Rationalization does not engage the conscience to a sufficient degree to modify the decisions being contemplated. Rationalization provides the excuse for doing things that make no sense, appear illogical, don't truly have a possibility of success or are wrong, but that have no guilt attached.

Principled Leadership;
A Balancing Act for a Lifetime

Principled leadership cannot separate the conscience from the decision process because the conscience is tied to the ability of the spirit to seek understanding and wisdom. Separating the conscience from the decisions we make simply defeats the purpose of doing the right thing because it is the right thing to do. Without conscience, we may very well never know what the right thing to do is. Staying true to the conscience is a singularly effective tool at remaining true to the overall values themselves, which is critical to successful principled leadership.

- Doable

The attributes of a good life are sometimes not easily found in our culture. The pendulum of our cultural focus appears to have swung too far towards the material human centric aspect of life. Because of this, the spirit has been marginalized, leading to an unbalanced culture.

Today, if you engage in the culture as it is, there is too much to take in and the key players appear to be the ones with issues or problems.

Principled Leadership;
A Balancing Act for a Lifetime

In essence, politics, news programs and most of the entertainment programs are based on negative characteristics.

This is not to say that there is no good in our culture today. When you take a moment to look closely at the individuals on the normal stage of living life in the community, you can readily find people who are demonstrating very good solid leadership characteristics. Even in entertainment there are plenty of movies and a lot of music that is uplifting and positive. It just seems to be at the national political level, or rather at what we should call the power level, where things get fuzzy.

The quest for power appears to defeat the quest for wisdom. On the national level the examples we have are many; from politicians who speak half-truths or falsehoods to get their way, to journalists who report bias as fact; to talk television and radio, where pundits talk endlessly about their perspective and create division where it does not exist and doubt when confidence is needed; to movies and television who glamourize the worst of human nature; we can easily see that national exposure, combined with the power it yields, defeats the quiet moment to gain understanding and wisdom.

These choices our leaders make, both elected and un-elected, lead our culture in a poor direction, as the national stage where our most significant leadership exists is also where so much of the impact and influence on our culture resides. This influence when leaning towards human centric values and temporal power tears the fabric of our value systems and pulls them apart, leaving people disenchanted, bewildered and eventually, defeated.

In order to counteract this decline, God provides us the principled leadership values that are necessary. In order to improve the leadership we have, principled leadership is necessary. With leaders living the values of principled leadership, we can positively influence our culture and shift the pendulum back to balance.

- <u>God Separated From Us</u>

Our nation was founded on a belief in God. The Declaration of Independence states:

Principled Leadership;
A Balancing Act for a Lifetime

"We hold these truths to be self-evident, that all men are created equal, that they are endowed by their Creator with certain unalienable Rights, that among these are Life, Liberty and the pursuit of Happiness."

This declaration clearly states that the founders of our nation declared that God was an integral part of our founding and belief. Here it clearly states that the "Creator" gave us rights, not a government body. This is very powerful and supports the idea that God was integral to our ability to succeed as a nation.

The issue non-believers raise is the issue of the interpretation of Article 1 of the constitution, which reads:

"Congress shall make no law respecting an establishment of religion, or prohibiting the free exercise thereof; or abridging the freedom of speech, or of the press; or the right of the people peaceably to assemble, and to petition the Government for a redress of grievances."

Principled Leadership;
A Balancing Act for a Lifetime

The interpretation many non-believers raise is based on the perceived separation of church and state this article raises. In their opinion, this article forbids any mention of God or any "religious" word or action at any time in any place or event that is considered to be "public money funded." However, their understanding is simply wrong.

The confusion stems from the interpretation of the phrase, "establishment of religion," as used in the article. By making it an argument that any reference to God is the establishment of religion, these individuals have managed to remove references to God from an incredible number of places. But what does the phrase, establishment of religion, actually mean?

Let's take a quick look at the definition of some words; establishment, establish and religion. Read the definitions through.

Establishment / noun
1. the act or an instance of establishing.
2. the state or fact of being established.

3. something established; a constituted order or system.

4. the existing power structure in society; the dominant groups in society and their customs or institutions; institutional authority: The Establishment believes exploring outer space is worth any tax money spent.

5. the dominant group in a field of endeavor, organization, etc.: the literary Establishment.

Establish / verb (used with object)

1. to found, institute, build, or bring into being on a firm or stable basis: to establish a university; to establish a medical practice.

2. to install or settle in a position, place, business, etc.: to establish one's child in business.

3. to show to be valid or true; prove: to establish the facts of the matter.

4. to cause to be accepted or recognized: to establish a custom; She established herself as a leading surgeon.

5. to bring about permanently: to establish order.

Principled Leadership;
A Balancing Act for a Lifetime

Religion / noun

1. a set of beliefs concerning the cause, nature, and purpose of the universe, especially when considered as the creation of a superhuman agency or agencies, usually involving devotional and ritual observances, and often containing a moral code governing the conduct of human affairs.

2. a specific fundamental set of beliefs and practices generally agreed upon by a number of persons or sects: the Christian religion; the Buddhist religion.

3. the body of persons adhering to a particular set of beliefs and practices: a world council of religions.

4. the life or state of a monk, nun, etc.: to enter religion.

5. the practice of religious beliefs; ritual observance of faith.

Trying to put together any understanding of religion as the means of establishing it as a government program is banned by the article. This is obvious and clear. So what would the establishment of religion mean if it were government mandated? It would mean:

- Mandatory worship within the established religion
- Mandatory participation within the established religion
- Employment based on religious participation
- Benefits based on religious participation
- No freedom to NOT worship
- Religious leaders only running for office
- Religious leaders only being selected for government positions
- Only the established or recognized religions could be followed

Clearly, none of these exist within our society, and never have since the founding of our nation. It is clear that these types of things would be contrary to the article. Yet still we push God out. It begs the question, is it establishing religion to:

- Allow prayer before a football game?

- Allow a nativity on city hall property?
- Leave "Under God" in the pledge of allegiance?
- Leave the Ten Commandments up?
- Allow Christian or other groups of school kids to meet on school property?
- Say a prayer before beginning an event?
- Using public property to support the morals and values of citizens?

I hope you agree that none of these actions, most of which have been banned by the courts, can conceivably be interpreted as "establishment of religion." So what is going on?

It is the systematic removal of those guideposts in life that enable people to hone and sustain their conscience. The conscience is the target, because the conscience requires a balance between the spiritual and physical reality to operate effectively. Degradation of the spirit through removal of references to God pushes the spirit out of the picture and enables those activities that feed on the physical aspect of life – raising the human to the supreme position of life. This is exactly the opposite of what principled leadership is about. If the human being is the apex of existence, then God cannot exist. If God cannot exist, then the foundation of our values cannot exist. If our values cannot exist, then we have human centric chaos and descent into anarchy.

This is the progression we must turn back or the cycle we must stop, and the only way to do it is through principled leadership.

- <u>So What Is It</u>

At the beginning of this book I said that we have something in common, which is an interest in leadership, but that I was especially interested in principled leadership. So what is principled leadership? What does it mean to live a life of principled leadership?

Living principled leadership is the establishment of a solid foundation based on the values found through faith and belief in God that supports a strong structure where a person can be courageous, seek wisdom, live virtuously and live in peace, knowing the life being lived has value. It is the act of not only being a leader in a family or an organization, but being a leader of self. It is not only leading for a moment in time, but leading one's self internally for all the days of life lived.

It is being the best you can be to your family, neighbors, friends, acquaintances, co-workers, bosses, employees and anyone else.

It is:

- Being honest with yourself and others.
- Telling the truth.
- Being considerate.
- Loving those you love and expressing it.
- Forgiving.
- Being joyous.
- Sharing.
- Caring.
- Being worshipful.
- Being humble.
- Being thankful.

It is living the virtues of life and loving life as a gift from a loving God, and sharing that same feeling with those around you. These are not hard things to do, when you get your "self" out of the way.

Finding that balance in life between the spiritual and physical is a significant part of principled leadership. Living in that balanced place gives you the foundation and strength to withstand life's issues. It is a balancing act, but one that is rewarding in the living.

The secret of living principled leadership is to have reverence and thanksgiving for the life we have. Doing this simple task releases the energy we store up to fight negativity or hold back or treat unfairly, and focuses it on the positive aspects of enjoying and sharing life.

Living principled leadership is not something you retire from.

Living principled leadership is the expression of the personal relationship between yourself and God, emphasizing the reverence within the relationship and the values, wisdom and characteristics you learn and display through that relationship.

Living principled leadership is how you live life, right now, always. Your motivation, thought process, purpose, direction, energy, words, deeds, what you give, take and do, all of it – right now this very second defines who you are.

Living principled leadership is living in the now with all of the character and reverences your body and spirit can focus.

Living principled leadership is a powerful force that builds energy as it is lived to provide for a sustained, positive focus for all the days of life.

Living principled leadership is a life time goal that is achievable, livable and doable. It takes commitment and energy.

Living principled leadership is taking the power of God's values and putting them to work in your life.

Principled Leadership;
A Balancing Act for a Lifetime

Bibliography

All definitions are from Dictionary.com.

All bible verses are from BibleGateway.com, New International Version.

Lucasfilm Ltd. *Yoda Bring You Wisdom I Will.* Shenzhen, Chronicle Books LLC, 2010.

Jackson, Glenn. *Growing Leadership; Managing Developmental Chaos.* Bloomington, IUniverse, 2008.

Andrews, Andy. *The Travelers Gift.* Thomas Nelson, 2002.